YOU TOO
CAN HAVE
An Amazing
LIFE

JOHN CHALKIAS

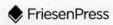

FriesenPress

Suite 300 - 990 Fort St
Victoria, BC, V8V 3K2
Canada

www.friesenpress.com

All scripture quotations taken from the Holy Bible, New International Version © 2011 by International Bible Society. Used by permission of Zondervan Publishing House

ISBN
978-1-5255-4075-2 (Hardcover)
978-1-5255-4076-9 (Paperback)
978-1-5255-4077-6 (eBook)

1. Religion, Christian Life, Inspirational

Distributed to the trade by The Ingram Book Company

YOU TOO
CAN HAVE
An Amazing
LIFE

Table of Contents

Forward

BY PASTOR BOB COTTRILL

For the past twenty-five years, I've had a ringside seat as John Chalkias has demonstrated what it means to live a principled life. Together with his wife, Susan, John founded the Seeds of Hope Children's Ministry, bringing practical help and hope to children and families who live on the margins of society because of poverty, politics, and disease.

How does something like this happen? Why are some people able to live an amazing life and step out of the ordinary to go places and do things that the rest of us only imagine? In this book, John sketches out a blueprint for a meaningful, victorious life as he reflects on the lessons and events of his own life.

When I first met John, there wasn't a lot to indicate what lay ahead of him; his education, finances, and background were nothing special. But even then there was something that set him apart: a commitment to integrity, a dedication to being a man of God.

I've walked alongside John over these past few decades, and I can assure you that these chapters are not just theories or second-hand ideas—they are life skills that have been tested in the rough and tumble of the real world. This book is a natural extension of John's life. The principles he outlines in these pages are the foundation upon which he's built his life and ministry.

Don't just read this book—study these principles and allow them to lead you into an amazing life anchored in God's truth and focused on loving and serving the people God has placed in your life.

Dedicated to Jesus Christ, who has lifted me out of the ash pit and seated me with princes. To Susan, the love of my life, who has made my life amazing, and to my children and grandchildren, who have blessed me with incredible joy.

With deep appreciation to Tami Strople, and Michelle Vandepol for all their help in editing the original manuscript.

Introduction
DEATH OF A CHILD

It was 2008 and my wife, Susan, and I were living at Grace Academy. Grace Academy is our orphanage/school, located in Zambia, for HIV infected or affected orphaned children. On this particular evening, it was past dark and my children, safe and healthy, were in bed asleep. A knock came on the door and I wondered who it might be.

As I opened the door, I found myself looking with annoyance at one of my construction workers. The first thought that came to my mind was, *He must want to borrow money or a tool.* Immediately I was filled with an attitude of inconvenience. I hate lending out tools. I'd like to think it was because I was very tired that evening that my attitude was so bad. I said his name and asked what I could do for him, but again with a terrible attitude.

As he began to speak, I noticed his eyes were full of tears.

"I need money," he said. "My daughter just died, and I need to buy a coffin." I wasn't expecting him to say these things. My mind shouted *WHAT?* as I stood there at a complete loss for words, the breath sucked out of me. Immediately, I felt sickened. Ashamed and convicted of my attitude and the way I had treated this man, my heart cried, *God, forgive me! What kind of missionary am I?*

Inviting him in, I asked, "What happened?"

"She had malaria," he said.

"But why didn't you come to me before she got critical?" I asked.

"We always get malaria," he said matter-of-factly. He was right. They often got malaria. His daughter had had malaria before and recovered, but this time her illness had rapidly worsened and before the family realized it, she'd become dehydrated and died. The first time I got malaria, I spent days in the hospital, where I received all kinds of medications and fluid intravenously. Despite the aggressive treatment and being a very healthy grown man, I still lost fifteen pounds. This little five-year-old girl didn't have a chance.

The next day, we went to the funeral house and paid for the funeral and burial. (Traditionally, family members will come from all over and stay at the family home, known during times of death and mourning as "the funeral house.")

The house was made of roughly-hewn bricks of clay that had been dug from the ground, molded, and then baked. Their floor was dirt. This home, as with all the others in this compound, had no running water. Water was fetched from nearby creeks in five-gallon pails, usually by the children and women of the house. The bathroom was a pit latrine out back. On the floor, in what might be called the living room of the funeral home, lay the body of the deceased little girl, wrapped in a tattered blanket. At the end of the funeral service, the family placed her frail body into the rough, panel board coffin and loaded it onto our flat deck truck, along with several wailing family members, and we slowly made the long drive to the cemetery. The name of the little girl we buried that day was Esther. She is the reason for this book.

I can't tell you how many children and staff we have buried since that day. The numbers are too many. Watching people struggle through life, living in deplorable situations, suffering and battling illness after illness, caused me to reflect deeply. I pondered hard questions like *What am I doing here? Is my being here making a difference?* As I reflected, it became clear that poverty cannot be eradicated by money alone. There has to be something more: a change in the mentality and beliefs of the people we serve.

Since then, I've started a program called ***Victorious Living.*** I use this powerful program as a tool to teach my staff and team members how to experience God's abundant life. I've put the principles used in ***Victorious Living*** together in a systematic way to create this book. Our goal as we work through the program is to empower those participating and to lift them out of their circumstances to a life of hope. Life circumstances vary. Sometimes people are born into situations that have perpetuated and cycled through generations, resulting in downtrodden people so burdened, there's no longer thought or consideration given to the possibility of a better life.

Through the principles outlined in this book and imparted in ***Victorious Living***, we try to teach good decision-making. In making one good decision after the other, a new pattern is created and generally leads to good results.

If you're trying to make your life better in your relationships, family, career, finances, and even in your emotional and physical health, then give this book a good read. In this book, I talk about God and faith. We are spiritual as well as physical beings, and there's a spiritual aspect to our physical being that must be included in our quest to better ourselves. To leave God out would be foolish. Everything we do has eternal value. Like the Gospel of Mark reminds us, "*What good is it for someone to gain the whole world, yet forfeit their soul?*" (Mark 8:36).

Jesus said He came to give us life and life more abundantly. This isn't a prosperity gospel. This book is written to help you be well and live a life full of hope and abundance. In order to reap full results and experience the changes in your situation, you will need to invest in yourself. Meditate on the principles discussed, make notes, study and review them regularly. Build new, healthy habits. I strongly suggest getting a journal in which to record your thoughts, prayers, actions, and results as you apply the principles you will learn. Put the principles I am going to share with you to work and ***You Too, Can Have an Amazing Life!***

Chapter 1
PRINCIPLE OF CHOICE

"Now choose life, so that you and your children may live"
(Deuteronomy 30:19)

The death of little Esther was, on many levels, the direct result of poverty. Death is a constant in Zambia because of HIV/AIDS, malaria, parasitical diseases, water-borne diseases, malnutrition, a poor medical system, extreme poverty, and the list goes on. This type of living and suffering in this day and age is unacceptable to me.

At the time of this writing, we have 172 children residing with us, and eighty full-time staff. That's 172 children's lives saved and eighty staff members who can feed and care for their children because they have steady employment. Yet the problems remain. *How do we keep our children from ending up living in the shanties and repeating the cycle of poverty? How do we help our staff raise their standard of living and climb out of poverty?* It's a problem that haunts me.

I've pondered the question: *What has made me different?* I've looked back on my life and wondered *What has kept me from poverty?* It's not that I deserve better than the folks I work with. I don't. As a young man I made some very bad choices and serious mistakes that would have led me down a road of poverty and jail.

So what changed my course? I can say my life changed the day I accepted Christ as my Savior. Everything changed: my morals, my health, my family life, my economics, and the way I thought. It didn't happen all at once, but I can definitely trace it back to that day of decision. I can honestly say that Jesus Christ saved me from a life of poverty. But the same thought puzzled me, because I can say the majority of people we work with in Zambia are Christians. *Why aren't they blessed? Why have they not been lifted out of poverty?*

I don't believe that when a person becomes a believer, he or she becomes wealthy or trouble-free. That simply isn't true. But when we accept Jesus as our Lord and Savior, the Holy Spirit dwells in us. We're given a new heart, and our thoughts, actions, morals, and outcomes should change to align with our new position in Christ. In other words, the way we live and our results should reflect our new faith and hope.

Our faith should lift us out of despair, fill us with hope, and change everything for us. Instead, what I found was that a person might have faith, but poverty of mind still prevailed, which brought poor results. This problem is prevalent in the West as well.

Why some people and not others suffer in poverty is a complicated issue without an easy answer. However, there are things every person can do to lift himself or herself out of poverty, hopelessness, and despair into a life of hope and joy. This is the reason for this book. In it you'll find principles that work for all people, in all cultures, and at all times. While this book is written with my friends and people in Zambia in mind, the principles will work for anyone trying to change their lives from being poverty stricken to victorious living.

Have you ever wondered why some people end up working dead-end jobs, addicted, bankrupt, homeless, in prison or in bad relationships, while others have a life of relative ease and success? I like how Andy Stanley describes choice in his book *Principle of the Path*. He states: "Direction, not intention, determines destination."[1] In other words, you might desire a happy marriage, but if you regularly leave your wife at home and hang out with your buddies in bars, you're heading in the wrong direction.

You might want to be wealthy but have a habit of getting into debt; you're heading in the wrong direction. You might want to be a champion athlete but would rather party with your friends instead of hitting the gym; you're heading in the wrong direction.

Where do you want to go? People on the wrong path often justify or rationalize their actions with "just this one time," or "no one will know," or "just this one drink." This is a slippery slope. To justify and rationalize poor choices and actions will lead you down a path that you don't wish to travel. Going down the wrong path becomes a habit.

A smoker remembers his first cigarette and how sick it made him and wonders how it became a pack-a- day habit.

---

1 **The Principle of the Path: How to Get From Where You Are to Where You Want to Be** by Andy Stanley—Published 2008 By Thomas Nelson. Pages 14,15

An alcoholic remembers the first time he got drunk and violently sick. He remembers emphatically stating "Never again," but now finds himself drinking every day. The first time someone gets involved in a criminal activity they're often scared and conscience-stricken. However, if they do it again, they find it becomes easier and easier. Before they know it, it becomes a way of life.

I know a man who, after the first time he committed adultery, cried over the guilt he felt for breaking his vows. Yet despite the anguish he felt the first time, he continued to commit adultery. Today, the same man tries to rationalize his behavior by saying he is a sex addict. In actuality, he chose to go down the wrong path repeatedly and created a habit. Multitudes have ruined their lives by choosing to do the same thing: to go down the wrong path repeatedly, creating devastating habits.

I understand that the principle of choice can be difficult to understand or accept. Some people are born into horrible situations or have something catastrophic happen to them. Some are born into abusive homes, others into extreme poverty, and still others are afflicted with physical disabilities and limitations. However, for each person there comes a time of decision to rise above any situation or to accept defeat.

Consider immigrants to North America. People have come out of extremely harsh conditions, war torn countries, and impoverished nations. Some fled persecution and discrimination and came without education or financial resources, but they made a decision and changed their lives and the lives of their descendants. They started businesses, bought homes, and prospered while many people born in abundant countries in North America live in poverty and lack. Have you ever wondered about this?

Throughout this book we'll talk about the principles of God and the need for you to make a decision. The secret to changing your life is that you need to change your life. Make the decision and stick to it. Choose this day whom you will serve. Choose your path. Make the decision.

You must make your intention your direction and stay the course no matter how difficult things get. If you do this, you'll arrive at your intended destination.

First things first: What do you want? Make your list; write it out. Read your list every day. Make it your goal. Do you want to start your own business? Do you want to be prosperous? Do you want a good marriage and family life? Do you want a healthy body? Do you want to lose weight? What exactly do you want? Think very hard about this.

Most people live life randomly without direction and without a plan and wonder why they can't have the life they dream of. Such a dream life requires a direction and a decision. Make the decision to change your life and stick to it. Make it your absolute obsessive, compulsive, driving desire. Think about it day and night.

Start now. Make a list of the things you desire for your life. What do you want spiritually? What kind of family life do you want? What kind of career do you want? What do you want financially? What do you want physically?

What makes us different from any of God's creatures is that we have a mind and we can choose. We choose our lives and how we live. This is a God-given principle. Your life is a matter of priority and decision. You might not think so depending on your circumstance, but I urge you to have an open mind and be ready to put these principles to work for you. If you really want to change your life, you have to make a decision. Let's start this exciting journey to an amazing life!

Chapter 2
PRINCIPLE OF FORGIVENESS

"And forgive us our debts, as we also have forgiven our debts"

(Matthew 6:12)

I think it would be fair for me to assume that you're reading this in an effort to better your life. After all, the book is titled, ***You Too, Can Have an Amazing Life***. This book is put together in a systematic way. This next chapter is a difficult one, and many might put the book down and not read any further because of the difficult subject. I encourage you to consider the thoughts in the following chapter.

Many people cannot change their lives because they feel they don't deserve better. They're burdened with guilt, shame, and worthlessness. They're convinced that this is their lot in life, that this is what they are worth and deserve, so they don't even bother trying.

I know that feeling. I grew up in a poor immigrant family, and everything was a struggle. I believed the rich were lucky and privileged. All around me, the people I knew were in poverty. I saw drunkenness, broken families, drug abuse, and crime. That was my norm, both my reality and my paradigm. Paradigm consists of your culture, habits, and way of thinking. We're going to talk about how to change it in a later chapter. At the time, my paradigm was making me angry, bitter, and guilt-ridden. Deep down I knew I wasn't living right.

The one thing I was good at was fighting. This led me into an amateur boxing career with the dream of going to the Olympics. When my dream didn't materialize, I found myself back to my old way of life. I was a very dedicated boxer and as long as I was training, I kept out of trouble. When I quit boxing, I found myself unraveling. In no time, I went from training several hours every day to my old lifestyle of drinking, smoking, and street-fighting. I even got myself arrested. At this low point I made a decision to change my life and leave the path I was on that was leading to a dead end. I really believed I was heading to prison.

In desperation, I decided to give boxing another chance, but this time as a professional. The night before my pro debut, I lay sleepless in my hotel room. In an attempt to stay my restless, excited, and anxious mind, I picked up the Gideon Bible from my nightstand and started to read. I really didn't understand what I read. It actually confused me more than anything.

When I returned home, intrigued by the reading I'd done at the hotel, I picked up my sister's New Testament and started reading about Jesus. As I read about Him I felt dirty yet at the same time drawn and loved by Him. Shortly after, I found myself on my knees, confessing to Him all my sins, all the things I'd done to hurt my family and others. I asked God to forgive me of the things I was so ashamed of, things that weighed so heavily on me. Immediately I felt the burden being lifted.

Another thing I did, which wasn't as easy, was forgive those who'd hurt me. This took longer to do. It was like "God, are you kidding me? You want me to forgive so and so?" I had to do this repeatedly, because I'd forgive a person then find myself still angry, or experiencing triggers that would set off memories, causing the anger to arise again. To forgive means to forgive from the heart and sincerely wish that person well.

You'll never be able to move forward without forgiving those who have harmed you. It doesn't matter how great the harm, you need to forgive. Your pain may be such that you feel entitled to hate. Perhaps you lost a loved one to violence and feel that if you forgive the one who caused the harm, you'll betray your loved one. I've seen many unfathomable atrocities committed against children; I understand how easy it is to hate the perpetrator. There is so much evil in our world.

There needs to be a time of forgiveness. I've heard it said that unforgiveness is like drinking poison and hoping the one you hate dies. Harboring unforgiveness will have worse effects on you and your life than on the one who has wronged you. Not forgiving will ultimately harm you more and ruin your life. The wounds are deep; the feelings of anger, bitterness, and shame run over and over in your mind, causing bitterness and robbing you of joy and even future relationships. Until you're able to forgive, the wrong and sin committed against you will always have power over you. You'll always be a victim and have the attitude and mindset of a victim. You can never be the victorious person you want to be as long as you're a victim. Forgiving makes you responsible for your own actions; you no longer allow what happened in the past to control your current situation.

Here are a couple of things to keep in mind. Forgiveness doesn't mean that you become a doormat or that you need to make up with the person who harmed you. Nor are you required to remain in an abusive situation. If you're currently in an abusive relationship, whether it's physical or sexual abuse, you need to get out. You need to talk to someone you trust and who can help you to safety and direct you to resources and the proper authorities.

Refusing to forgive fills you with negative feelings that will sabotage your growth and the changes you want to make in your life. They may even hinder future relationships. Unforgiveness is also detrimental to your health. Among other things, it causes:

- depression
- anxiety
- stress
- weakened immune system
- blood pressure abnormalities
- anger, resentment, and bitterness in every relationship
- reduced enjoyment of your present life because you're living in the past
- a sense of meaninglessness or lack of purpose
- an inability to develop deep relationships with others
- disruptions in your prayer life and relationship with God

While forgiving those who have harmed us is important, it's equally important to forgive yourself, especially in cases of sexually abuse, as young victims often carry an overwhelming sense of misdirected self-guilt, shame, and responsibility. In situations like this, it may be necessary to involve a professional counselor.

We've all made mistakes or bad decisions, failed, or done things we're deeply ashamed of. We can experience a deep sense of guilt that is paralyzing. We need to forgive ourselves in order to move forward.

We all do wrong and fail at times. Sometimes we do things maliciously. Another part of forgiveness is asking others to forgive you for something you've done that has caused them pain. This requires you to humble yourself and ask for forgiveness. In some cases, you'll need to make restitution; however, there's no guarantee that the offended person will forgive you. You'll need to give them room. Just because you're ready to ask for forgiveness doesn't mean they're ready to forgive. You can do little in a situation like this besides pray for them.

Another aspect of forgiveness concerns the culture, environment, or hierarchy into which you were born. You may have feelings of resentment and hatred towards those who exploited your community and people. Without forgiveness, the feeling of being a victim will keep you under its power.

Pick a quiet place in your home, someplace where you won't be disturbed. Think back to when you were a child and the teacher who humiliated you in front of the whole class and how you felt. Think of that bully who made you dread going to school. Think of your specific situations. They may have formed your character, the way you feel about yourself, your self-confidence, self-worth, and even the way you look at other people. In this quiet place, go back in your mind to these events and forgive. Speak words of affirmation to yourself as a child and encourage yourself with words of truth. Recognize that any words or actions that made you feel inadequate or defeated are lies. Believe the words of God: that you are precious in His sight, you were fearfully and wonderfully made, and He has a marvelous plan for your life.

Finally, we might even have to forgive God. God doesn't sin or make mistakes, but sometimes we blame Him for our circumstance and the tragic events that happen to us, such as the death of a parent or an illness in our lives. There will come a time—in heaven if not before—when we'll know why God allowed certain things to happen. If you can't accept His sovereign will at this time, forgive God and go on in faith that He loves you!

Forgiveness is a process that needs to be done daily. It may be difficult, but it's liberating! God's greatest gift to you is forgiveness; your greatest gift is to forgive. This gift is so amazing because it not only gives you a clean slate in this life, but also eternal life.

"For God so loved the world that He gave his one and only Son, that whoever believes in Him shall not perish but have eternal life" (John 3:16).

God loves us so much, He gave His Son so that we won't have to face judgment. We are all sinners. We have all failed. But God gave His Son as a sacrifice to take our punishment.

Jesus did that on the cross, even though He was innocent. He committed no sin, yet He took our punishment so we can be declared innocent in God's eyes. To receive this gift of forgiveness, all we need to do is accept it by faith. As the scripture above says, "… *whoever believes in Him shall not perish but have eternal life.*"

If you would like to experience God's forgiveness, let me lead you in a prayer:

Dear God, I believe in Your Son, Jesus. I thank You that He took my sins on the cross. I confess I am a sinner and I repent of my sins. I give You my life and pledge to follow You. Amen.

You may ask, *Is that it? That's all I have to do?* I know it sounds too simple, but there's nothing more we can do to make us worthy of God's love. There's nothing we can do to earn it or to deserve it. In and of ourselves, we will never be good enough. The only thing we can do is accept God's salvation, because He's the only one that can make us holy.

Christ's salvation enables us to live a life of forgiveness and in forgiveness, and be amazing!

Chapter 3

PRINCIPLE OF GOING THE EXTRA MILE

"If anyone forces you to go one mile, go with them two miles"

(Matthew 5:41)

When Jesus spoke these words, His listeners understood exactly what He was talking about. They might not have understood why He said such a thing, they may have even hated what He said, but they knew exactly what He was saying. Under Roman impressment law, a Roman soldier passing by a Jew could order him to carry his pack for one Roman mile (milion = 1,000 paces).

Imagine being back in the Bible days. You've just brought your sheep to market after a very long walk from the meadow where they were penned. Exhausted and dusty, you're tired but happy and relieved to have enough money to live on until the next flock is ready to sell. You're walking up the path, happily minding your own business, when you notice him walking towards you. You look left and right, hoping to avoid him, but it's too late. He's already seen you. His eyes pierce you with his stare. He sneers and then he barks out the words you dread: "You, Hebrew! Carry my pack!"

With that he drops it with a loud thud onto the dusty path. With great difficulty, knowing there's no choice, you hoist the hundred-pound pack over your shoulder and begin the tortuous journey. Your heart fills with hatred and anger. With every step the back of your legs burn under the weight. You constantly have to adjust the load as different muscles in your back and shoulders cramp up. You curse him in your mind as he shouts for you to move faster.

Then, all of a sudden, you remember the rabbi you heard the other day on the mount. He spoke about going the extra mile. He spoke about loving your enemies and many other things that seemed so paradoxical. None of it made sense, but He was so intriguing. When He spoke, you felt the presence of God. Your mind swirls with thoughts about what to do with the rabbi's words when the soldier's shouting brings you back to reality.

"That's far enough," he says.

You walked the mile. You sigh with relief, but then words came out of your mouth that shock you.

"Sir, may I carry this a little farther with you?"

At first he mocks you. In your mind you're thinking, *Man, that was a mistake.* But compelled, you carry on. A little farther down the road, the soldier looks at you and for the first time isn't shouting.

His face is softer as he asks, "What is your name? Why are you doing this?"

Then something strange happens on this walk. A conversation unfolds. You notice that he's young, about the age of your son. He's missing his home and doesn't want to be here. His name is Anthony. You find out that he's on his way to meet his detachment and then to Damascus on a new assignment. At that moment you both become human. There's a respect that wasn't there before. And now you understand why Jesus said those things, because there's very little reward for doing what is required. It's only after doing more than what's required that walls are broken down, barriers are removed, and relationships are formed in deeper ways.

How do we apply this principle today? It's been my experience in the work force, both as an employee and employer, that most people do just enough at work so they don't get fired. These same people do this while complaining about their wages, the company they work for, and life in general because they can't get ahead. Going the extra mile gets you noticed and in line for a promotion. It wins you favor, whether it be in employment, academics, or relationships. If you want to change your life and your position in life, you need to do the extras others aren't willing to do.

Nobody likes a complainer. In contrast, when you do something extra, people appreciate you. It makes them grateful for you and they want to do something in return. Going the extra mile gets you noticed. It sets you above your peers and elevates your status.

Here is a man who is wretchedly poor. He is extremely anxious that his surroundings and home comforts should be improved, yet all the time he shirks his work, and considers he is justified in trying to deceive his employer on the ground of the insufficiency of his wages. Such a man does not understand the simplest rudiments of those principles which are the basis of true prosperity, and is not only totally unfitted to rise out of his wretchedness, but is actually attracting to himself a still deeper wretchedness by dwelling in, and acting out, indolent, deceptive, and unmanly thoughts.

– James Allen[2]

Keep up your efforts, even if your boss is a tyrant who takes advantage of your goodwill. You're increasing your personal value as an employee. God may have another opportunity in mind for you. You may be offered a position with a competitor or have opportunity to open your own business or … the possibilities are endless.

Ultimately, we aren't working for man but God. He will reward each man accordingly. The Bible is full of examples of people going the extra mile. My favorite story is of Joseph, who even though he was a slave to Potiphar and later to the jail master, always went the extra mile. Because of his service, God not only freed him but elevated him to the position of second in command of all of Egypt!

---

2 From the book **As A Man Thinketh** by James Allen— Published 1903

The principle of going the extra mile works in our family life, in our neighborhoods, in our churches, and in our friendships. Go the extra mile with goodness and sincerity in your heart. Seek the good of others.

> Whatever you do, work at it with all your heart, as working for the Lord, not for human masters, since you know that you will receive an inheritance from the Lord as a reward. It is the Lord Christ you are serving.
> (Colossians 3:23–24)

Related to going the extra mile is *"doing the things failures hate to do."* This might be considered going the extra mile for yourself. In 1940, Albert E.N. Gray wrote a speech titled, "The Common Denominator of Success." Albert Gray took it upon himself to study and find out what made successful men successful. He wanted to know why some men succeeded while other men with the same (or better) qualifications failed.[3]

He discovered that the common denominator shared by all successful people was that they formed the habit to do the things that failures hate to do. They don't like to do those things any more than failures do, but they're driven by purpose. He went on to explain that everyone has purpose to better their life, to support their families, etc. However, these purposes aren't strong enough for most people, as they

---

3 **The Common Denominator of Success** by Albert E.N. Gray Speech at the 1940 NALU (National Association of Life Underwriters) annual convention in Philadelphia.

find it easier to adjust to the hardships of poor living rather than to the hardships of a better life.

To prove it, he went on to say, "Just think of all the things you are willing to go without in order to avoid doing the things you don't like to do. All of which seems to prove that the strength which holds you to your purpose is not your own strength but the strength of the purpose itself."

Successful people are driven by their desire for good results. Failures are driven by the desire for easy methods and are satisfied with the results of doing the things that require the least effort. In other words, failures look for instant gratification, whereas successful people find gratification in pursuing their goals and the good results that will accompany their efforts.

Think of the things you hate to do that could lead to successes in your life. They may include getting up early to prepare for the day, studying and learning new things on your own time, cold-calling perspective clients, etc. List them and make it your habit to do the things that will ultimately pay you back in dividends.

Make it your habit to do more than is required. Make the decision to go the extra mile and be amazing!

Chapter 4
PRINCIPLE OF THINKING

"No one stops to think ..."

(Isaiah 44:19)

To expand a bit on the scripture above, God is looking at His people, the Israelites, and asking with anguish in His heart, *Can you not think?* They have turned from the living God to worshiping metal, stone, and wood crafted into idols.

In idol worship, a man takes a tree, fashions half of it into an image, and worships it. The other half he uses as firewood to keep himself warm and to cook his food. How can he consider this piece of wood to be his god? How can he pay homage to it? Can he not reason that he made it, and it has no power? Yet a whole nation did this exact same thing. They didn't stop to think! Sounds so stupid, doesn't it? Yet it happens all the time to this day. Superstition, cultural traditions, peer pressure, family expectations, rituals, habits, and things that are not understood are practiced with unquestioned loyalty.

This occurs without any thought to whether a certain practice is beneficial to the well-being of the individual or community, or even if it's true. People are like sheep being led astray by belief systems without giving any thought as to why they do what they do.

A person's belief system is called a paradigm. A paradigm consists of a set of subconscious behaviors that are deeply embedded and guide people to act automatically without thinking, like a train on a track. Even if the conductor (conscious mind) wanted to go left or right, the train can only go where the tracks (sub-conscious mind) lead. The paradigm directs and controls your direction, your decisions, your relationships, your health and your economic situation.

This is the way cultures are formed. Culture is good when you consider music, dance, food, and beautiful traditions. Paradigms are passed down for generations and can have serious consequences. Consider, for example, female circumcision, sexual cleansing rituals, and caste systems. In this book I will focus on paradigm from the perspective of individuals, not entire cultures. Consider the following:

One day a daughter asked her mother a question as she watched her prepare a roast. "Why do we cut the ends off each side of the meat before putting it in the roasting pan?"

The mother replied, "That's the way you're supposed to do it."

"Why?" the daughter asked.

The woman thought about it and said, "This is the way my mother taught me."

Curiosity welled up in both of them, so they phoned the grandmother and asked, "How do you prepare a roast?"

"Well," the grandmother replied, "first I prepare a rub with olive oil and spices."

"No, Mom," the woman interrupted. "Why do you cut the ends off the meat?"

There was a long pause on the line and then she finally answered. "I don't know. That's the way my mother taught me." Great-grandmother was living in a nearby nursing home, so they phoned her and asked. She replied with great reminiscing that when she first got married her roasting pan was too small, so she needed to cut the ends off the meat so that it would fit in the pan. Great-grandmother had to cut the ends off for necessity, but the following three generations blindly did what they saw without asking why.

This is a cute anecdotal story, but this type of behavior without thinking can have huge consequences. To ask why is one of the highest forms of learning, because it involves critical thinking.

These are very important questions to ask yourself: Why do you do what you do? Why do you live where you live and in the type of house you live in? Why do you work where you do? What do you talk about every day? What do you constantly think about? Make a list of your questions and answers. The last two questions will determine the answers to the previous ones, because what you think and talk about reflects your paradigm. Your paradigm, because of presupposed and sub-consciously set limitations will determine where you live, what you do for work, what you earn, and your lifestyle.

Here's an example: Joe was raised in a family that always struggled to make ends meet. Many of the conversations in his house centered on lack. He constantly heard about bills, debts, and the fear of being out of work. As an adult, these are the kinds of things he still thinks about and experiences.

Think of the conditions of growing up in a broken or abusive home. What kinds of things would an impressive young mind hear repeatedly? The words and ideas we grow up with are stored in our subconscious mind, which defines our reality, our paradigm. We think and act and live accordingly. If you think like a poor person, you'll live like a poor person. If you think like a victim, you'll be a victim. The opposite is also true. If you think as a successful person, you'll be a successful person. You can control the programming of your paradigm. To change the way you live, which will determine your future, you must change your paradigm.

> Don't look at your present circumstance, "There is nothing in a caterpillar that tells you it's going to be a butterfly."
> —R. Buckminster Fuller

How do you change your paradigm? You first have to take note of your way of thinking, talking, and living. Ask yourself why you think and do the things you do. Be honest with yourself. You might be shocked!

Secondly, ask yourself what you want. Decide what you want. Write it down. Do you want to be successful? Do you want a better career, a better family life, or a closer walk with the Lord? Do you want to do great things for God? Then you need to change the way you think. Take the word "can't" out of your vocabulary, because when you use that word, you've already decided the outcome. Get excited about your plans, your dreams, and the changes you want to make. Our conscious mind thinks emotionally and logically. When your emotions and logic are in agreement, it's easier to change the programming of your subconscious mind.

Consider the following scenarios. Have you ever watched a tragic love story on TV and found yourself crying? Have you ever watched a crime drama in which the villain was so evil, you found yourself seething with anger and hatred? As you sat there, you could feel your body tense and the adrenalin rush through your veins. Do you watch or read the news and get upset about currents events, whether it's about the government, the economy, or even your favorite team? Have you ever stopped to consider how these images and things you're hearing affect your body?

Simply hearing bad news can make you tense, angry, afraid, or depressed. Unintentionally, you allow these things to affect you in a negative way. Often these things aren't even real but the product of someone's imagination. Bad news makes great headlines, and Hollywood knows how to rile you up emotionally.

If bad news or fake images on a screen can cause that kind of stress or fear, imagine what happens to your body when you listen to negative things every day. Negative things can seem unavoidable: a co- worker complaining about the company, a relative badmouthing another relative, or a neighbor doing or saying about you that makes you angry. What happens if you do this every day? If you repeatedly allow things outside of yourself to make you angry, resentful, or depressed, then you allow these feelings to form your personality.

It should be the other way around. How we feel on the inside should affect how we see situations on the outside. Fortunately, we can choose our thoughts, and we don't have to accept bad news or gossip. We can choose to see the good in every situation. The thoughts we choose create our character, circumstance, and reality. If negative thoughts can alter our minds and even our bodies, then the opposite is also true: positive and loving words can make us strong, well, and happy. The following words were written over two and a half millennia ago by King Solomon in his book of wisdom: "*Gracious words are a honeycomb, sweet to the soul and healing to the bones*" (Proverbs 16:24).

Up until a few decades ago, scientists believed that, after childhood, the brain ceased developing. However, neuroscience has shown that the brain continues to develop into our old age. This is great news! We can grow our intelligence and expand our imagination. We can reshape our destiny simply by changing the way we think. Through the power of thinking, you can reprogram your sub-conscious mind.

You can change the way you've processed your life experiences and the things others have taught you. You can change your paradigm. You can reprogram your mind to think differently and to have limitless potential. Your brain has the ability to form and reorganize synaptic connections in response to learning new things. This ability is known as neuroplasticity. The brain can change itself, re-wire itself, and actually grow. As you practice the things you learn, you strengthen the new neuron connections, which will now dominate old connections or old ways.

Think about the life you want. Think of the person you want to be. Make it a reality in your mind first. Play that reality in your mind over and over until you're actually living it. Everything starts in the mind. Everything that was ever created started in someone's mind as an idea.

> Do not conform any longer to the pattern of this world, but be transformed by the renewing of your mind.
>
> Romans 12:2

Learn to think big. Remove limitations from your thoughts. Replace negative thoughts and words with something better, something that excites you, and something you really want for your life. Change the way you think and the way you talk, and your life will change. This needs to be done with passion and deep desire. Decide today to change your way of thinking, your thoughts and words. Be amazing!

Chapter 5
PRINCIPLE OF FAITH

> "'Have faith in God,' Jesus answered. 'Truly I tell you, if anyone says to this mountain, "Go, throw yourself into the sea," and does not doubt in their heart but believes that what they say will happen, it will be done for them'"
>
> (Mark 11:22–23)

The Bible tells us that without faith it's impossible to please God, because anyone who comes to Him, must first believe that He exists and that He rewards those who earnestly seek Him (Hebrews 9:6). It's by faith we are forgiven and given a new start. This in itself is the biggest paradigm shift that can happen in a person's life, because as the Bible says, we become a "new creation." We think differently, we act differently, and we live differently.

I believe each person must have their own faith and moment of conversion rather than living off the faith of others. For example, you might have grown up in a Christian home and gone to church, prayed, sang hymns, and done all the *Christian things* because that's the way you were raised. This isn't necessarily a bad thing; however, it's your paradigm and you're like a train following the tracks that have been laid in your sub-conscious by others. Unless you have wrestled with your beliefs actually struggled with why you believe and what you believe and ensured that your relationship with Jesus Christ is in place, you won't experience the power of faith.

Consider faith. Consider the greatness of God who created us as His highest form of creation on earth. He gave us a free will to choose. He gave us intellect and imagination. He gave us creative powers that have allowed mankind to develop incredible technology, like computers, cell phones, and microchips. He gave human beings the intellect that developed technology that enables us to travel at incredible speeds. Besides the convenience of automobiles, we can now travel on bullet trains, supersonic jets, and spaceships. We have technology that allows us to perform organ transplants and laser surgeries, and develop artificial limbs. Consider this God who is so great that He created the universe with such order and precision that our world can sustain life despite the incredible mathematical improbabilities.

Scientists are concluding that the universe is the result of intelligent design. Look up to the stars, the sun, and the moon. Look upon the majesty of the mountains and rivers and oceans. By the law of physics, nothing can be without a cause. The law of mathematics tells us that nothing plus nothing is nothing.

All creation testifies of the greatness and power of our God. If you walk on a beach and observe the beautiful ridges made in the rock and sand by thousands of years of the ocean beating against it, you might conclude that it's evolution at work. However, if you walk a little farther down the beach and see etched in the sand a heart with an arrow going through it with the words "John loves Susan," you'll conclude that an intelligent being created it. Millions of years of the ocean beating against the sand can never produce a heart with these words. This is a simplistic form of creation but can never happen by chance, which is what evolution is. Consider the laws of physics and thermodynamics, all the sciences, and the evidence of nature. God who created the universe created you in His image, with a mind that can think and create. He gave us the ability to change our world, to change our circumstance, and to do amazing things. To do these amazing and incredible things, He gave us the power to believe.

Jesus said, "As you believe, so shall it be done to you" (Matthew 8:13, paraphrased). The power of faith allows you to live a victorious life above any circumstance. Even in the midst of suffering there can be incredible joy, peace, and victory. By faith we are healed. By faith we ask in prayer, and in faith we receive. By faith we move mountains that are impossible for those who do not have faith. By faith we see things that are unseen and bring these into reality. By faith we have the power to change and have amazing lives.

Jesus said that He came to give us life and life more abundantly. By faith we receive and experience this abundant life. Everything changes by faith, and nothing great ever happens without faith. You may not agree with me. You might say that many great things have been done by men without faith in God. The Bible says that He sends His rain on the wicked and the righteous. In other words, the laws and principles of God work for believers and unbelievers. Gravity is a law of physics and it works for everyone. You may not believe in the law of gravity, but if you step off a cliff, you will demonstrate it. Physical laws and spiritual laws are the same but are in effect in different dimensions. Men who have done great things, made great discoveries, developed amazing inventions, built magnificent buildings, created incredible wealth, and led nations did so by faith. Whether it was faith in God or themselves and their own power or intellect, they had faith to do what they did.

The man with faith in God taps into the power of the Almighty.

> Faith is the defeat of probability by the power of possibility. The prophets dreamt the improbable and by doing so helped to bring it about. All the great human achievements, in art and science as well as the life of the spirit, came through people who ignored the probable and had faith in the possible.
> —Rabbi Jonathon Sacks

Where are you placing your faith? The Bible says the righteous shall live by faith. Live by faith and be amazing!

Chapter 6
PRINCIPLE OF WORDS

"The tongue has the power of life and death, and those who love it will eat its fruit"

(Proverbs 18:21)

Most people don't realize the power of words. Words have the power to create and destroy. The Bible teaches that God created the whole universe and everything in it by speaking. He said *"Let there be light, and there was light"* and so on. In John 1:1–3 we read; *"In the beginning was the Word, and the Word was with God, and the Word was God. He was with God in the beginning. Through Him all things were made; without Him nothing was made that has been made."*

Jesus is the Word of God; however, there's more to this scripture. In the original Greek, "the Word" is translated *logos*. *Logos* actually means two things: the spoken word, and thought. We get the word "logic" from *logos*. If you read the verse again with this understanding, it means that in the beginning, God through His thoughts and ideas spoke all creation into being.

We've been created in God's image and possess attributes of the Almighty. What we think and really believe, we speak into being—whether for good or bad. If we continually speak negative things, negative things will happen. If we speak positive things, positive things will happen. Unfortunately, we tend to pray for or speak positive things in our serious conversations, but in our causal everyday conversations, we talk negatively. This reflects our true character. Take note of what you talk about with your friends, co-workers, and neighbors, because most people don't realize the things that come out of their mouths. Do you find yourself complaining about your job, your wages, and your lack? Do you complain about the government, taxes, or the economy? Do you find yourself complaining about your spouse, your kids, or family? Do you gossip about your neighbors or friends? The Bible says you are speaking curses into your life. You are cancelling out your prayers for good by speaking doubt and negative words. Jesus said that what comes out of the mouth of a man is what makes him unclean, because with our words we speak what's in our hearts or our subconscious mind.

Words not only have power over your life but on others as well. The way you speak to others either lifts them up or tears them down. Words bring encouragement or despair. Words bring fear or courage. How do you speak to your acquaintances, your family, and your children? Are you speaking blessings to them? Do they leave your presence with joy and encouragement, or do they leave feeling deflated?

> "Don't mix your words with your mood, you can change your mood but you can't take back your words."
> —Anonymous

Pakashan is a young man who grew up at Grace Academy and now works for us. We raised him from a toddler after his parents died. Growing up, he always struggled in school and wasn't academic. After school I hired him on the construction crew, and he has worked for us ever since. A few years ago, I was laying out a wall we were building, and Pakashan was working with me. We were having a conversation about life in general, and somehow the subject of money came up. I asked him how he was doing financially.

"Not so good," he said.

"Do you have money in the bank?" I asked.

"No," he replied.

"Why not? You have a full-time job. What happens to your money?" I asked.

He explained that his rent was very high and he had to buy food. Whatever was left over was used to support his grandparents.

"Why don't you buy a house?" I asked.

"I can't afford it."

I explained that if he didn't buy a house, then thirty or forty years later, he'd still be renting and making someone else wealthy, and he'd still have nothing and be saying he couldn't afford it.

"YES! You can afford to buy a house," I responded. "Why don't you move in with your grandparents and save your money so that you can buy a house?"

He thanked me for the advice and we went on to different jobs on the site. About a year later, I was working on a scaffold when Pakashan climbed up to see me.

"I did it!" he exclaimed excitedly.

"Did what?" I asked.

"I listened to what you said. I bought a property and I'm building a house!"

I'd forgotten all about our conversation the previous year. I was so happy for him. That week he took me out to see the property and what he was doing. He was so proud of himself. It took him about a year to complete, and he was proud to report to me that his house was rented and making him an income.

"Okay," I said, "now do it again. Buy another house and rent it. Then do it again. You'll be making more money from your rental income than you do working for us. You'll only come to work because you like me so much," I joked.

Pakashan is currently completing his second house. It was a word of encouragement that changed the projection of his life. He also stopped saying "I can't" and started asking "How can I?"

How do you speak words to yourself when your mind tells you that you're not worthy, or good enough, or smart enough? How do you respond to this? Consider carefully how you talk about yourself. How many times do you say "I can't"? For example: *I can't change. I can't lose weight. I can't learn this or that. I'm not talented, or strong enough, or brave enough.*

The Bible says, "*I can do all things through Him* [Christ] *who gives me strength*" (Philippians 4:13). That scripture provides great affirmation. Speaking scripture to yourself is very powerful, as you're speaking in agreement with God's Word. Are you feeling guilty? The Bible says you're forgiven. Are you feeling weak? The Bible says let the weak say I am strong. Are you poor? The Bible declares you rich. There are hundreds of scriptures declaring victory and blessings for your life.

Finally, understand that words form your reality. With your words you tap into God's abundant grace, power, and riches, which are in endless supply! Intentionally train yourself. Watch what you say and make it your practice every day to speak words of affirmation to those close to you and to yourself. Speak words of life and blessings and be amazing!

Chapter 7
PRINCIPLE OF AGREEMENT

"Again, truly I tell you that if two of you on earth agree about anything you ask for, it will be done for them by my Father in heaven. For where two or three gather in my name, there am I with them"

(Matthew 18:19-20)

I want to be very clear as I write the next chapter, God calls us to love all people. We're not to look down on people but to love, respect, and care for everyone, especially the weak, the poor, and the vulnerable. We are to have compassion and genuine concern for those considered to be the outcasts of society. This is what Jesus did, and this is what He calls us to do. We have a calling to serve. Later we'll talk about generosity and love; however, in this section we focus on self-development and the need to get ourselves healthy in all aspects of our lives, including spiritually, emotionally, mentally, physically, and financially.

If you're serious about changing your life and your standard of living, and if you're putting the principles we've been talking about into practice, you will face resistance.

This can come from the people you're closest to and the people you spend the most time with. If people oppose you and try to discourage you, they do so because they're being true to their way of life, their habits, and their beliefs, which make up their paradigm. They cannot relate to your plans and aspirations. They might even think they're helping you and it's their duty to bring you back to reality.

If you take the five people you associate with the most and are most comfortable with, and average their income, your income will be within 10 percent of that average. Why? Because your paradigm dictates who your friends are, what you earn, where you live, and the type of life you live. If your friends, the people you spend most of your time with, are successful, chances are you too are a successful person.

> The righteous choose their friends carefully, but the way of the wicked leads them astray.
>
> (Proverbs 12:26)

Consciously and subconsciously you will glean off each other's ideas, beliefs, words spoken, and actions taken. If the people you associate with are wealthy, chances are you too are wealthy. If, however, your friends are struggling financially, you too will be in the same proximity financially. If your friends use filthy language, talk negatively about their circumstance, and use alcohol and drugs, then your behavior will be similar to theirs, because this type of life is your reality. This is your comfort zone. This is the crux of the matter: you have become comfortable.

The good news is that as you better yourself, as you strive to improve on your character, then you will be attracted and attractive to people with similar aspirations. But it takes courage. I've known people who live in extremely poor conditions, but as bad as their conditions are, they are comfortable there. Their life is all they know, and as much as they talk about wanting to change and wanting a better life, without realizing their need and power to change, they never will.

Having a spouse or a close friend who is in agreement with you to encourage you makes all the difference. A husband and wife team striving towards a goal with unity is a very powerful thing and almost always meets with success. Another powerful ally is a mentor. Find someone who is already living the life you want. It could be someone in your church, business, or circle of acquaintances. Make it your goal to get close to someone you respect and want to emulate. Don't be afraid to ask for advice.

Be courageous. Stop associating with toxic people and people who tear you down. Make the decision to better your life and to associate with those who can help you do this. Being in agreement with a small group of people with similar goals is very powerful. Surround yourself with people who are passionate and have vision, who are intelligent and make smart decisions, and who are courageous and have a positive attitude. Nurture connections with people who believe in you and make you feel alive and energized because of their attitude and encouragement. And be the same positive blessing for others.

Most importantly, surround yourself with people who will build you up and with whom you're in agreement spiritually. This is the final point, because when you're united in prayer and in agreement with God's Word, the Lord is in the midst of you. Now we're talking about supernatural power! With a small group of people, you can change your life, community, and the world! The Christian faith started with a small group of committed, united men and women, and the world hasn't been the same since!

As you are bettering your life, find someone who will stand with you—a friend, a mentor, and especially your spouse. Find someone who will pray with you and for you … and be amazing!

Chapter 8
PRINCIPLE OF PERSISTENCE

"But the seed on the good soil stands for those with
a noble and good heart, who hear the word, retain it,
and by persevering produce a crop."

(Luke 8:15)

Persistence is the test of faith. It's the ability to believe in
spite of the appearance of failure. It's the courage to keep
going when confronted by overwhelming obstacles. It's
the will to hold on to dreams and aspirations in the face of
apparent impossibilities and improbabilities. It's the belief
in yourself and your dream despite what the crowd says.
It's the strength to keep going through pain and suffering, because defeat is not an option. It's the ability to pray
unceasingly when it seems like your prayers are only bounc-
ing off the ceiling. It's persevering in hardships.

When the breakthrough finally comes, the triumph of
whatever you achieved will be so much more appreciated,
because whatever comes to us easily and without effort is
taken for granted and not valued. Whatever it is that made

you suffer or was your obstacle or barrier will make your achievement great.

I've had the great privilege of meeting many people who have encouraged and inspired me by their courage and persistence. One of them is a young man who, just by his very presence, inspires me with his courage, enthusiasm, and persistence. Anderson was born to a poor family in a village in northern Zambia. When he was born, the villagers told his parents they must kill him because of his deformed legs and feet, which were considered an abomination. Others suggested he must have his feet cut off.

"He is cursed," they said.

His father refused, declaring, "This is my son!"

Anderson was born with an elephantiasis-type disease. His feet and legs were grossly enlarged. His father was a farmer. He loved him and protected him. One day while in the field, he collapsed and died. This was devastating for Anderson. His dad, the man who loved him, protected him, and cared for him was gone. In addition to that, family members claimed everything his father owned, leaving Anderson, his mother, and his siblings destitute. Traditionally in Zambia when a husband dies, all his property, including household goods, is claimed by the paternal side of the family.

As Anderson grew, walking became extremely painful. His mother had a basket made and put on the handlebars of her bicycle. She'd put Anderson in it because he was getting too big to carry. He says he remembers the pain caused by his legs dangling from that basket. Even more painful were the jeers from other boys as they rode by. They would curse him and throw stones at him. As he got older, Anderson went to live in a village for handicapped children.

School wasn't easy for him, because his painful feet made it difficult to learn comfortably. He was advised to remain home and elevate his feet to lessen the pain, but this would mean quitting school. Anderson didn't take that advice. School was the only option he had if he was going to have any future. Anderson admitted that his situation at times made him feel like he was walking in a dark, endless tunnel. His future seemed dark and uncertain, and his pain seemed endless. He was in tears most of the time due to his pain, but he never gave up and he continued to work hard in school. He had the strong spirit of persistence.

I was taken to meet Anderson by Mission Medic Air, an organization providing medical care to people in remote areas without medical services. We had to fly into the village, as it was far removed from any city or highway. I was taken to the school and given a tour, and then Anderson was brought to me. As he walked towards me, he kept his head down, because he was ashamed of his feet. I could tell each step he took was painful. Even though I was told his feet were large, I was shocked by how big they were. It never occurred to me that he would be barefoot because his feet were so big, he couldn't fit in any shoes. They had brought Anderson out of his room to meet me. That's where he spent most of his waking hours. His feet caused him enormous pain, so he didn't do things other boys did. The only things he enjoyed were reading and studying.

We were able to bring Anderson to Ndola, the city where we are based and run Grace Academy. We brought him to the children's hospital, the adult hospital, private clinics, and mining hospitals. Then we brought him to the teaching hospital in the capital, Lusaka, where we thought for sure they would be able to help him, because they had international professors and doctors teaching there. However, all the doctors said the same thing: "Amputate the legs above the knees." This was something I couldn't do. I just couldn't bring a sixteen- year-old boy to the hospital and pick him up the next day with no legs.

When I first brought Anderson to Ndola, he was hopeful that finally he was going to get some help. But after all the hospital visits and the doctors' recommendations, he too was ready to concede to amputation. It helps so much when someone reaches a low point and there seems no way out to have a friend who still believes. I guess at this point you can say I was the one being persistent.

I kept up my search for help for Anderson, and I was able to connect with an organization called OMNI in Virginia that could house and arrange Anderson's corrective surgeries. He had to have multiple surgeries over a period lasting eight months. During his stay in Virginia, he lived with the president of OMNI. She was a nurse, and her husband was a doctor. All their friends and people they associated with were in the medical profession. In addition, Anderson became close to his surgeon, whom he saw every week. Through these relationships, an interest in medicine was sparked in Anderson.

When he returned to Grace Academy in Ndola after his surgeries, we had a large welcoming committee to meet him at the airport. We were waving flags, beating drums, and singing songs. Anderson had arrived home wearing shoes!

Anderson completed high school and then was accepted at Apex Medical University in Lusaka. As of this writing, he's in his fifth year studying medicine. It hasn't been an easy road. He still suffers from pain, walking is still difficult, and standing long hours is very hard on him. He was born into a community that didn't think he should live. He was raised by a single mom who lived in extreme poverty. He was sent to a village of handicapped children to be forgotten and was told that he shouldn't have legs. But somehow this young man got it into his mind to be a doctor, and through persistence and sheer will power, he will be. I can't think of a doctor who will have more patience, empathy, and compassion than Anderson.

Another person who inspires me is Pastor Lu, an amazing man I'm privileged to work with in our Asia projects. He's a well-educated man, but rather than go into business, he and his wife chose to live in the shanty slums of Yangon to minister to the poor and share the gospel. His Buddhist neighbors didn't like hearing the gospel message, so they threatened him, reported him to the police for proselytizing, and threw stones at him. Pastor Lu never retaliated. He just prayed and loved them more. He and his wife prayed and asked God how they could reach their neighbors with the gospel.

They noticed the women in the area getting up early every morning to get water and carry it back to their homes for their daily needs. The Lu's home was the only one with running water in their area. That was an answer to prayer, as they realized that providing water was one way to serve their neighbors. Every day Lu would fill the five-gallon pails for those who needed them. His wife started a preschool, teaching the children in their area for free and sharing the gospel with them.

When the cyclone Nargis hit in 2008, most of the bamboo homes in their neighborhood were destroyed. Pastor Lu was able, with the funding from Seeds of Hope, to provide food, water, and medical care for seventy people and rebuild twelve homes in his neighborhood. He currently leads an overflowing house church in his home for many of the people who once stoned him!

I can tell you many more stories of our kids who came to us near death, suffering from the grief of losing their parents, rejected by family, malnourished, suffering from HIV/ AIDS and other diseases, and experiencing the emotional upheaval that comes with situations like these. Yet now they are thriving in university, studying to be engineers, doctors, and teachers.

Be persistent with your dreams and your calling. Don't let failure and obstacles stop you. What is it that you really want to do? Write it down, read it to yourself day and night. Put these principles to use. Be persistent and be amazing!

Chapter 9

PRINCIPLE OF BEING FAITHFUL IN THE SMALL THINGS

"Whoever can be trusted with very little can also be trusted with much, and whoever is dishonest with very little will also be dishonest with much"

(Luke 16:10)

Isn't it remarkable that people think they can skim a dollar here and a dollar there in small matters but be trusted with large accounts? If they're not honest in small amounts of money, how can they be trusted with large amounts? Being faithful in the little things is God's apprenticeship program. You must do, or learn to do, the little things before you go on to bigger things. Our honesty and integrity in money also reflects our attitude in other things as well. Do you take shortcuts and expect great results? Character is measured by how well we can be trusted. What do you do with the little things?

Many people say, "If I was wealthy, I'd be generous." The fact of the matter is, if you're not generous with a little, you won't be generous even if you're wealthy. Generosity has nothing to do with how much you have. Someone might say, "If I was famous, I'd speak up for those who cannot speak for themselves." But again, social justice doesn't depend on those who are famous. If you want to do great things for God, you must be faithful in the little things. How we treat our money and our time has to do with what's in our hearts.

This is true in every area of our lives. Doing great things is a popular ambition, whether it's to be a great champion or a famous musician, a great business leader or a wealthy entrepreneur. Everybody wants to be great. But to be great, you need to be really good at the little things. They are usually the things nobody else notices.

Some examples of these things are getting up at six o'clock in the morning to practice every day for years, working a full-time job and then writing music or practicing until two o'clock in the morning and doing small gigs on the weekend every day and every weekend for years. It means working seven days a week, twelve hours or more a day, to make your small business succeed. One day when you own franchises, people will think you're an overnight success, but there's no such thing. It takes years to be a success. Nobody becomes an overnight success. It takes many mistakes, risks, sacrifices, and hard work. It also requires treating each customer well. It means taking care of the small details, caring about quality, and being faithful in the little things.

I learned in boxing that fights aren't won in the arena on fight night. They're won in the gym by practicing combinations over and over, thousands of times. It takes hundreds of rounds of sparring, miles and miles and miles of road work.

It is repetition, repetition, repetition! There are no crowds cheering, no applause, no cameras, no trophies or belts. It's just you in a stinky gym hitting the heavy bag. But you do it with determination, passion, and dreams.

It's the same with everything. You only get out of life what you put in, day in and day out. Doing the little things that may not be noticed turn into big things that are. If you can't do the little things, you won't be able to do the big things.

Everybody wants a good marriage and a good family life, but few people consider that it's the little things that make all the difference. Everybody wants to have a passionate sex life and the glow of romance in their marriage. Marriage's reality is that 90 percent of your time with your spouse is spent doing the mundane things: laundry, shopping, chores, mowing the lawn, taking kids to soccer games, taking the dog for a walk, and making lunches. It's how well you do these everyday things that keep the spark in your romance.

Nothing takes the romance out of marriage faster than taking the other person for granted, so do these things with passion, do them together, and do them with a loving sparkle in your eyes. One of the things I really enjoy doing with my wife is cooking together. What can I say… I am Greek! The kitchen is where the magic happens for us.

Other little things that do great work in your marriage are practices like sending a loving text message in the middle of the day, tucking a love note under the pillow when you leave the house, or calling in the afternoon to say how much you love your spouse.

If you get the small things right, the big things fall into place. This includes how you wake up and greet your wife or husband, whether you tell them you love them every morning, kiss them, put on the coffee or tea for them. It emphasizes the importance of listening to them and looking for opportunities to serve them. It's good practice to reflect on what your conversations are like at the dinner table and how you greet them after a hard day at work. Even beyond the words you choose, the tone you use is important.

It's good to stop and think. Are you reflecting love and appreciation, or a demanding and critical attitude? The same goes for thinking about your interactions with your children. How do you speak to them every day? Are you loving and kind, day in and day out? How are they going to remember growing up in your family? It's the repetition of your kindness that will make all the difference in your relationships. When you think about it, the small things aren't small at all. It's doing the small things that matters.

Being faithful in the small things also means doing the right thing when no one is watching or noticing. Things like making sure the car is in good condition for your spouse, making sure the house is safe every night and that the doors are locked and the stove is off. Even though everyone is sleeping, you make sure that they're safe. You check your children's bikes to make sure the brakes are in good condition and the tires are full. Don't begrudge them if they don't notice. This is the whole point. You're not doing it to be noticed or recognized but out of genuine love and concern.

The same applies at the work place. There are opportunities everywhere. It happens when you go into the restroom and clean the mess on the floor. It happens when you arrive early and notice a messy staff lunch room and clean it before everyone gets there. It could be a small gesture like putting a fresh coffee pot on for the next shift. They may be things that no one sees, but you do them with kindness in your heart. But God sees them and orders things right in your life. What you sow always comes back to you. That's a spiritual law.

As you consider this principle, think about where you're already practicing it and build on that. Thank God for opportunities to serve others. What small things are you letting fall through the cracks? What can you be doing better? Think about this, pray about this, and ask God to show you areas in your life where you need to take care of the little things. Make a list and purpose in your heart to take care of these things. Read your list every day. Do the small things right. Do them with passion. Do them with love. Be faithful in the small things and be amazing!

Chapter 10
PRINCIPLE OF BEING GRATEFUL

"Jesus asked, 'Were not all ten cleansed? Where are the other nine? Has no one returned to give praise to God except this foreigner?'"

(Luke 17:17)

The scripture above describes ten men who had leprosy and came to Jesus requesting to be healed. Because of their disease, they were considered outcasts and unclean and lived in areas away from other people. Leprosy is a horrible disease. An infected person develops lesions over all their body and they lose sensation in their fingers, toes, and limbs. Often they lose digits or limbs because they don't feel pain when they injure themselves.

When these men came to Jesus, they kept their distance and shouted their plea. Jesus instructed them to go and show themselves to the priests, who would declare them "clean" as was required by the law. As they went they noticed that their leprosy was gone, but only one returned to give thanks. Their lives, their future, and their well-being changed in an instant, but they weren't grateful. I can't imagine why these men at the moment they realized they were healed wouldn't be jumping for joy and thanksgiving. Perhaps bitterness, self-pity, or anger gave them an attitude of entitlement.

I can almost hear the disappointment in Jesus' voice as he asks, "Where are the other nine?"

Part of the joy of giving is seeing the joy in the receiver of the gift. It encourages us to continue giving. You can say joy begets joy. When the receiver doesn't express joy or gratitude, it makes the giver almost reluctant to give to that person again. Not that we should look for recognition each time we give, but we all like to be appreciated.

Have you ever thought that God likes to be appreciated too? I'll be bold enough to say that when we give thanks, God listens. He doesn't listen to you when you complain and whine. I believe that as you realize your blessings with gratitude, He will open the windows of heaven and rain more blessings on your life.

Have you ever had a deep desire for something that you thought would bring you much joy, enrich your life, and bring you contentment? It might have been a dream to get married and have children. Perhaps it was a desire to own your own house. When you were very young, it might have been the anticipation of getting exactly that toy or bike you dreamed of on Christmas morning. As a teenager, it may have been a coveted sports car. It could be any number of things. You fill in the blank. However, that thing seemed out of reach. Maybe you couldn't afford it, or it didn't seem possible to ever achieve it. Eventually, you put the thought out of your mind. Then unexpectedly, someone gave you that exact item you so desired. Do you remember that feeling of a longing fulfilled? That feeling of overwhelming joy and being valued is called gratitude.

We don't always have that feeling of gratitude. We spend most of our lives taking the most important things in life for granted, and most of those things are free. They include our lives, our health, and our very breath. We rarely reflect on these things. We do the same with the people in our lives: our family, our spouse, our children, our friends and co-workers. We seem to feel that they'll always be there. Have you ever taken the time to count your possessions? I think you'd be surprised to know how much you actually own. I hear people say this all the time when they're moving: "Man, I didn't know I had so much stuff!"

In contrast, on several occasions I've been in people's homes where there were no possessions— no furniture, no appliances, no lights, and no bathroom. All the clothes they owned they were wearing and would wash every evening. Besides a couple of pots and plates there was nothing else, not even a chair to sit on. It's a very humbling experience when someone living like this is full of joy and so hospitable that they offer you a plate of the little they have to eat. It's also an honor and a blessing. Gratefulness is amplified by their sacrifice. If you have a home and possessions, stop right now and give thanks. Reflect on what your life would be like without these things and give thanks for them. What happens when we take things for granted? When we neglect to give thanks, we don't appreciate the things and people in our lives, or even realize the gifts we've been given, and we miss out. We don't experience the joy and contentment that come with the gifts.

> Gratitude is the healthiest of all human emotions. The more you express gratitude for what you have, the more you likely you will have even more to express gratitude for.
>
> –Zig Ziglar

Gratitude is an awareness that we've been blessed. It means noticing that we have all that we need. It's seeing the cup half full, seeing the good in any situation. The psalmist David was full of gratitude, for he wrote *"my cup runneth over"* (Psalm 23:5, KJV). Not only did he see his cup half full, but he said it was overflowing with God's blessings! This is the strange phenomenon that happens as you see the good in all situations. When you look on the good, you focus on it. And what you focus on becomes your reality. All of a sudden, you realize all your blessings, and your cup truly overflows.

> It is not happy people who are thankful. It is thankful people who are happy.
>
> –Anonymous

Two people can be in the exact same situation, but one is living in despair and the other in hope. What's the difference? Being grateful, even in gloomy situations, changes your attitude and the way you see things. Being grateful makes you more optimistic, which makes you more resilient.

Look for the good in the situation no matter how bad you initially think it is. You will find good in it. The Bible teaches this principle when it says, *"give thanks in all circumstances*" (1 Thessalonians 5:18). If God is telling us to give thanks in all things, it means we have a choice. We can be grateful or gloomy. We can see God's hand in the situation and trust Him, or we can live in worry and fear. If we chose the latter, we'll miss out on the joy and victory that come with trust. Worry is the polar opposite of gratitude. It's not seeing the blessings and the grace being offered to us.

Being grateful is good for your health because it relieves stress. Grateful people are more enthusiastic, more energetic, and more fun to be around. Because grateful people have a positive attitude, people like them more, they network better, and they're more likely to succeed.

In the beginning of the book, I suggested that you journal as you go through these principles. Start each day of your journaling by making a list of five to ten things you're grateful for. What a great way to start your day! Decide right now to consciously be grateful. Say thank you more often and mean it because you truly consider what you have and what's being done for you.

Have an attitude of gratitude and be amazing!

Chapter 11
PRINCIPLE OF BEING GENEROUS

"Give, and it will be given to you. A good measure, pressed down, shaken together and running over, will be poured into your lap. For with the measure you use, it will be measured to you"

(Luke 6:38)

A few years back while I was living in Zambia, we knew an artist named John who painted murals on many of our buildings. On this particular morning, I was on the building site when John came by the office to see me. He sat in the nsaka (a grass thatched roofed building like a gazebo) while he waited for me. He lived in a township outside the city of Ndola and it must have taken him over an hour to walk to Grace Academy.

That morning I was dealing with a contractor who'd failed to deliver as promised. The building he'd erected wasn't built right, the workmanship was poor, and the materials used were substandard. It was going to cost a lot of money to correct all the mistakes and rebuild most of it. I was dealing with a few other staff issues that morning as well, so I wasn't in a good mood. I asked God why I was there and why I had to deal with such dishonest people. That whole morning as I went from one situation to the other I carried an attitude of self-pity and complaining. I was being so judgmental and self-righteous.

About noon, I had to go into town to get supplies, and I remembered John patiently waiting for me. I asked him if he'd mind meeting with me in the car as I drove. That way I could also drive him home and save him the walk.

The conversation in the car was just pleasantries and I wondered why he'd wanted to meet with me. I figured he must have just wanted a ride back to the township. As I pulled over to let him off at his destination, he told me he was grateful for what we were doing for orphaned children and that he wanted to contribute to the work. He then handed me an envelope, which I put into my shirt pocket. I thanked him as he closed the door and walked away. I didn't think much of his gift as I drove off. I thought maybe he'd given me a card with a prayer in it, because he only earned a few dollars a day. It wasn't until much later that I looked in the envelope. As I opened it, I saw to my amazement that he'd given a full month of his earnings to the ministry. John lived in poverty in a home the size of my garage. His gift was made at a great sacrifice to himself and his family.

I was instantly humbled and cried out to God to forgive me for the terrible attitude I'd sported that day. That day God taught me humility and the power of a generous gift that I still think of often. John's gift gave me such encouragement that I wasn't alone, and it gave me an appreciation for my staff that I didn't have before. I think every gift offers encouragement that the receiver isn't forgotten in his plight or desire.

In the last chapter I noted that gratefulness not only makes you feel good, but it's also good for you. I think it's safe to assume that being generous is also good for your health, for Jesus said that it's more blessed to give than to receive.

Many people feel uneasy when asked to give. That's a shame. Mistrust, greed, or the fear of lack makes them lose out on the privilege of being generous. I love one of the core values in our church: **"We will give with irrational generosity."**

Jesus wasn't embarrassed to talk about giving. He didn't feel bad asking people to give up everything and follow Him. Whenever He asked for anything, He offered something far greater in return. This is the law of giving: it always comes back to you multiplied!

Paul wrote, "*Whoever sows sparingly will also reap sparingly, and whoever sows generously will also reap generously*" (2 Corinthians 9:6). Think about planting a seed. After the germination period, the seed will sprout, grow through the ground, and continue to maturity and produce fruit. Each plant takes a different amount of time to reach maturity, but once it starts bearing fruit, the fruit will be multiplied. In the same way, being generous has a germination period and a time to reach maturity. At the right time it will come back to you multiplied.

Generosity is a natural by-product of gratefulness. Paul wrote that "*God loves a cheerful giver*" (2 Corinthians 9:7). A generous person possesses an attitude of gratitude and gives out of the abundance in their heart. A stingy person thinks of their needs and has an attitude of lack and a hesitancy to trust.

This brings me to the next taboo subject: the tithe. In the Old Testament, the people of Israel were commanded by God to give the first tenth of their crops and earnings to the House of God. In addition, God wanted the best of their flocks and crops. This was to be an act of worship and to care for the priesthood and the poor in the land. However, the commandment came with the most incredible promise: "*'Test me in this,' says the Lord Almighty, 'and see if I will not throw open the floodgates of heaven and pour out so much blessing that there will not be room enough to store it*" (Malachi 3:10).

The tithe is a controversial topic for many people. Some say it's a bygone commandment, as we're no longer under the law but under grace. Others say they can't afford to tithe. To me, the tithe is an act of faith, and the promise along with it has been shown to me over and over. To those who say they can't afford to tithe, I say they can't afford not to. Tithing means putting God first. People always seem to have money for what's important to them.

Tithing will order spending aright, because it puts God first. When that happens, you won't be spending on frivolous things or going into debt. That's the first blessing. The second blessing is supernatural: God will meet your needs and provide riches without adding any trouble to it. Jesus said it best when He said *"seek first the Kingdom of God and then all these things will be added to you"* (Matthew 6:33).

Generosity can come in many forms. It can take the shape of giving of our time and our talents. For example, you could be a mechanic who fixes the cars of the elderly and single moms in your church. You could be a tradesman or a seamstress who can fix things for those on a fixed income needing assistance. Many people volunteer their time to feed the poor or to coach sports teams.

Generosity can also look like words of encouragement to someone who is feeling lonely, down, or discouraged. It could be as simple as donating goods like furniture or clothing. I recently learned of an interesting way Judaism has broken giving into eight levels. I think we all give in all eight ways or levels at different times and for different reasons; however, understanding these levels has certainly challenged me to aim for the highest level and for the right reasons.

EIGHT LEVELS OF GIVING IN JUDAISM

LEVEL EIGHT: Giving grudgingly is considered the lowest forms of generosity. The donor might have given because of guilt, shame, or obligation, but a gift is still given.

LEVEL SEVEN: Giving less than you can afford but still doing so joyfully.

LEVEL SIX: Giving generously but after being asked.

LEVEL FIVE: Seeing the need and giving before being asked.

LEVEL FOUR: The recipient knows the donor but the donor doesn't know the recipient.

LEVEL THREE: The donor knows the recipient but the recipient doesn't know the donor.

LEVEL TWO: Giving anonymously, where the donor and recipient do not know each other.

LEVEL ONE: Helping someone stand on their own. This preserves the dignity of the recipient and helps them to be independent, to be able to help themselves and eventually others.

If I could add to this list, I'd add giving at great sacrifice to yourself. This type of giving can only be driven by love. I've seen many parents go without food and clothing so that their children wouldn't have to go without. The story of John the artist is another good example.

You may never have thought about the principle of generosity before, but it's a joyous way to live. It's also an adventurous way to live, because God shows up in the most marvelous and unexpected ways to meet your needs. It boosts your faith and makes it stronger. Be generous and be amazing!

Chapter 12
PRINCIPLE OF COURAGE

"Have I not commanded you? Be strong and courageous. Do not be afraid; do not be discouraged, for
the Lord your God will be with you wherever you go"
(Joshua 1:9)

As God was leading the children of Israel to the Promised
Land, most didn't want to go. They wanted to return to
Egypt. God promised them a land flowing with milk and
honey, and they wanted to return to slavery. As miserable
of an existence as that was, they wanted to go back. Why?
They didn't believe God. They were afraid. They were comfortable with the devil they knew.

It's easy to do nothing, but it takes courage to change
your life. It takes courage to stand against the crowd, against
your friends and family, and against your former way of
life. It takes courage to change the way you think. It takes
courage to step out of your comfort zone. If you want to
change your life, to succeed, to be prosperous, to have the
kind of family you dreamed of, and to grow spiritually,

then you'll need to make the changes you know you need to make.

We started Seeds of Hope Children's Ministry in 1995 after Susan received a letter from a missionary in Thailand asking for help to start a home for HIV/AIDS orphaned children. At that time, thousands of children were dying in over-crowded and understaffed orphanages. It was at the height of the epidemic, and people were afraid of the disease. They didn't know what it was, and the stigma was devastating to children. HIV orphaned children were laid on rubber mats and received no human touch. The only touch they received was through latex gloves. They were hosed down with garden hoses to be cleaned. Children died because of neglect. In reality, 80 percent of them were HIV negative. They might have tested positive at birth because of their mother's antibodies in their system, but it takes approximately two years for a baby to develop their own antibodies. At that time, a true reading can be taken.

In 1995, we started the first home in that country for HIV orphaned children. It was a home where lives were saved. For those who succumbed to the disease, they were comforted and loved to the end.

As that home became sustainable and other organizations came alongside to help, we asked God where we could go next and where the need was greatest. The answer came through a dream Susan had: Africa. That same day, we were introduced to a pastor in Zambia, sub-Sahara Africa, the epicenter of the disease.

After two years of writing to this pastor, I boarded a plane to Zambia, leaving my wife and kids behind. Not knowing what to expect, my goal was to start our next project. As I sat on the plane, I wondered if I'd lost my mind. I'd never been to Africa before. I wasn't sure how to even start a project there; however, after two years of talking about it, both planning and fundraising, commitments were made, and the momentum was already set. There was no turning back.

In the beginning, Zambia was difficult and emotionally devastating. We lost so many children, staff members, and friends. But we also saw many miracles: children who were not expected to live survived and thrived. Several of them are grown now and in university. Some have already started their careers. The amazing realization for us was that what we once considered a sacrifice turned out to be the most incredible life journey.

When Susan and I first got married, we never in our wildest dreams imagined going to Asia or Africa, or meeting the people we've met, learning the lessons we've learned, or seeing the sights we've seen. We've witnessed miracles and family blessings we never expected. It was scary at first, as we didn't know what we were getting into. We had small children and had just moved into a new house with a big mortgage. We had responsibilities and every reason to say no.

I once asked Susan what she thought life would have been like for us had she not said yes to opening the first children's home. Her answer was profound: ***"Life would have gone on as always for us and we never would have known the difference."***

Dear friend, as you read this book, may I encourage you to live the amazing life you dream of. Take that courageous step to be different. Change your way of thinking. Stop your excuses, your reasons of why it's not possible. What is God calling you to? What has He gifted you with? What do you really want? What is holding you back?

Maintaining the status quo doesn't take any courage. Doing nothing but dreaming of something different won't change anything. Complaining doesn't make things better. Accepting your situation is not the answer.

Acknowledge that making the change to better your life is scary. If it wasn't, it wouldn't require courage. With courage, look into your heart. What is it that you want? Do you want a closer relationship with God? Perhaps you desire a better relationship with your spouse and children. Do you want to help more people? Do you want to lose weight or get in shape? Do you want to make more money or achieve a better career? Do you want to go back to school? All these things are good and more than possible. As long as what you seek is within God's moral laws and is right, God will give you the victory you desire. God wants you to succeed. He is the God of victory! He has courage for you. In turn, you need to do your part.

Make the changes in your life so that your *"future you"* will thank you! Be courageous and be the amazing person you were meant to be!

Chapter 13
PRINCIPLE OF LOVE

"Anyone who claims to be in the light but hates a brother or sister is still in darkness. Anyone who loves their brother or sister lives in the light, and there is nothing in them to make them stumble"

(1 John 1:9-10)

In 1997, we went as a family to the Agape Baby home in Chiang Mai, Thailand—the home we helped start. This was our first time there. As we were getting ready to go, I tried to prepare myself for what we might see. We'd already lost children to the HIV virus. We were going for three months, and I thought that the chances were high that we might have another death. I wondered how I would react.

When we arrived at the home we were taken on a tour. Children surrounded us as we went from room to room. Each one wanted to play or hold our hands or be held. Then we went into the nursery. As we walked by one crib, a baby caught my eye. She was absolutely emaciated and looked like a little concentration camp prisoner. I instinctively picked her up. I don't think she weighed more than one pound. I could feel every bone in her rib cage and spine. She felt like glass, and I was afraid I would break her. Holding her and looking into her face took my breath away. It felt like my heart stopped beating. I had to literally make myself breathe.

Her eyes looked right through me. They just stared with no expression whatsoever. She didn't blink or turn her head. She just stared into space. I asked Jane, who was showing me around, what was wrong with her.

"Failure to thrive," she answered.

What does that mean? I'd never heard that term before. She explained that they got her from the hospital where she was fed by a tube going into her head. No one had ever held this little baby or touched her. No one loved her, so she gave up. I remember talking to her and thinking, *How can anyone not love her?* That evening while we were having dinner and my children were playing around the table, I was still in shock and couldn't get that little baby out of my mind. Early in the morning we got the call that she'd passed away. She didn't die from AIDS or any other disease. She died being starved of love.

We were created to love God and each other. Think of the joy of love. It's the strongest emotion that God has blessed us with. Think of the joy of romantic love. Think of the love you have for your spouse. Think of the joy of your family around you. The sound of your children laughing gleefully is the sound of love in your ears. Reflect on the love of your parents. Give thought to the love of your family and friends. Think of the security a baby feels in its mother's loving arms. Think of the power of love and what people have done in the name of love, even to the point of laying down their lives.

Love gives us confidence and self-worth. Love makes us feel alive. It's energizing and it gives us strength and hope.

Without love, the opposite is true. We were created to be loved. Without love, we die. Our spirits are crushed. We are robbed of security and joy. We don't develop emotionally. We don't feel hope and trust. We are afraid. The world isn't a kind place. Without love, we die spiritually, mentally, and physically.

Our prisons are full of men and women who were starved of love. Our psychiatric wards are filled with people who were starved of love. As we strive to better ourselves, let us learn to love. Let's not hold back love from those closest to us, especially our children. If you were denied our most basic need, love, then turn to our heavenly Father, who will pour out His love to you. Pray right now and ask God to show you His love. Go to a quiet place and soak in His love. Learn to walk in His love. Believe and rest in Him and His love for you.

All of God's laws, commandments, and principles are related. Forgiving, going the extra mile, being faithful in the small things, thinking, believing, being generous, and being grateful are all intertwined. They all boil down to the two most important laws: *"Love the Lord your God with all your heart and with all your soul and with all your mind. This is the first and greatest commandment. And the second is like it: Love your neighbor as yourself"*—Jesus (Matthew 22:37–39).

With this in mind, learn to love. Take time, stop taking for granted those who are close to you, cherish every moment, serve at every opportunity, and show up to every event. Cheer every victory, encourage and lift up at every defeat. Be there for the ones you love!

I can think of no better way to end this chapter than with the Bible's most famous verse about love.

"*Love is patient, love is kind. It does not envy, it does not boast, it is not proud. It does not dishonor others, it is not self-seeking, it is not easily angered, it keeps no record of wrongs. Love does not delight in evil but rejoices in the truth. It always protects, always trusts, always hopes, always perseveres*" (1 Corinthians 13:4–7).

Learn to love this way. Love deeply, love dearly, and love freely. Let those close to you know you love them daily. Tell them at every chance.

Love deeply and be amazing!

Chapter 14
PRINCIPLE OF PRAYER

"Do not be anxious about anything, but in every situation, by prayer and petition, with thanksgiving, present your requests to God"

(Philippians 4:6)

I have an incredibly powerful tool that fits in the palm of my hand and can do the most remarkable things. Its signal actually goes to space and bounces back to me with all the information that I ask of it. In my parents' day and age, it would have been said that to do this would be impossible. Even when I was growing up, today's conveniences were the stuff science fiction was made of. Yet today everyone, even in third world countries, seems to have this tool. It's called a smart phone!

With it I can call from Africa to people in America in real time and hear them as clearly as if they were in the next room. I can do my banking. I can send money, emails, photos, and videos in high definition. Isn't it amazing that you can actually send a video in the air?

It can also tell me where I am and where I want to go by using GPS. It has a compass, a flashlight, a calculator, and countless apps. I can access over one million books on it. All this is done wirelessly. It works invisibly. With it, information flows through the air. Very few people in the world can actually explain how it works. To everyone else, it's a marvel, and no thought is even given to its miraculous powers. It's taken for granted.

There's an even more amazing tool we can all have, something more powerful than a cell phone. It too sends a signal to the highest heaven and comes back with amazing results. Not only is it wireless, but we don't even have to speak. We can think our requests in our minds! It's called prayer.

Prayer gives us access to the throne room of the Almighty. The amazing thing is, God our Father wants to hear from us. He rejoices when His children come to Him, just like you and I take great pleasure when our children come to us. Jesus said, *"Which of you, if your son asks for bread, will give him a stone? Or if he asks for a fish, will give him a snake? If you, then, though you are evil, know how to give good gifts to your children, how much more will your Father in heaven give good gifts to those who ask Him!"* (Matthew 7:9–11).

Jesus modeled prayer. If we want to know how to pray, we just have to look at Him. He always prayed. He was in constant communication with God. That's what the Bible means when it says we should be in ceaseless prayer. Jesus was always aware of God's presence and direction. This state of mind was never shaken by His circumstance.

He took time to pray, often going away to lonely places. Whether early in the morning or late in the evening, He always made time to pray. He knew the power of prayer. He received comfort in prayer. He prayed expectantly. He prayed with thanksgiving. He prayed with authority and power. He prayed trusting that God's will is best. He has given us this authority when we pray in His name.

Being in ministry for almost twenty-five years, I've seen amazing and miraculous things happen as a result of prayer. I've learned to depend on prayer. On a personal level and as an organization, we start every project with prayer.

People always ask, "How did you end up in Africa?" We'd never thought of going to Africa, but our prayer was, "Lord, where do you want us to go?" We prayed that prayer for over a year. Our initial thought was to start a new project in Thailand or in Asia, because we had so many contacts there and it made sense for us. The other thought was Central America, as this was closer and less expensive for us to travel to. Again, this all makes sense, right?

However, God gave Susan a dream that we were going to Africa. That very same day, we were introduced to a Pastor in Zambia. It took another two years to start that project. It's been my experience that we pray for something and we start moving towards that goal, but many times it's not what we think. The plan changes but the goal remains the same.

In our thinking, we never would have thought of going to Africa. It's a huge continent. We didn't know any one there and we wouldn't have known where to begin to even think about going to Africa. God's plan was bigger than we ever could have imagined! I find that happens in prayer often. We pray about something and it seems that nothing is happening, then all of a sudden, we get the answer in a way we never would have dreamed possible. Over my years in ministry I've learned to pray about everything and start walking towards that goal. You don't need to know how it's going to happen. It might seem impossible, but this is where you step back and let God do His thing. He is the God of doing the impossible!

Make it a habit to pray every day. Ask God to lead and guide you. Ask Him to protect you and your family. Ask Him to provide for your needs. Ask for wisdom. Ask for favor. Ask for forgiveness. Ask for grace and patience. Ask Him for victory over sin in your life and the things you're struggling with. Go to Him with all your problems, with all your sicknesses, and with all your worries.

Take time to pray every day and see amazing things happen in your life!

Chapter 15
PRINCIPLE OF SOWING AND REAPING

"A person's own folly leads to their ruin, yet their heart rages against the Lord"

(Proverbs 19:3)

The laws of physics state that for every effect there must be a cause, and for every action there must be an equal and opposite reaction. In agriculture, what you sow is what you reap. In other words, if you plant apple seeds, you're not going to reap oranges. This is also a spiritual law. Our thoughts and actions are seeds which will produce a harvest of the same kind. Our thoughts dictate how we live our lives, and how we live our lives gives us our results.

You can tell where people are headed by the things they do day in and day out. Repeated actions and thoughts become a habit, which becomes a way of life. Our lives are mostly lived subconsciously. Earlier we learned this is called a paradigm. More importantly, we learned that we can change ours.

Come with me, if you will, to the future. Yes, that's right. Step into my time machine and let's go meet your future self. You see, everything you do today will affect your future self. Every choice and every action will have a consequence, whether good or bad. God has given us this amazing thing called free will. With it we make choices every day. It could be to grow, to learn, to better ourselves and everyone around us, or to do the opposite. The possibilities and probabilities created by free will are endless. Every choice you make adds to the possibilities and probabilities. This is all a gift from God, and He delights in you making right choices and trying to reach for your potential. I say "trying" to reach your potential because I don't think anyone comes anywhere near reaching their potential, because it's so great!

Along with the gift of choice is the consequence. On our first visit, let's go visit you a few decades from now after a life of continued bad choices. Remember, a bad choice could simply be doing nothing. We walk inside the machine and buckle ourselves in. The door shuts automatically with a loud metallic noise and the machine starts to vibrate. The high pitch noise is painful to our ears, but the machine stops in a very short while. It seems like we didn't even go anywhere.

Upon opening the door, we realize that we're in a different place. It's dark and cold, and as our eyes adjust, we see that we're in a jail cell. A man is sitting on the bed. His face is worn, and his eyes are sunken into his head. His hair is unkempt. In a moment of unbelief, you realize it is you. He is broken and lonely and full of regrets.

He begins to explain to you all the choices you made and how it brought you here. It began with the conniving, the short cuts, the cheating, the stealing, and the using of people to get what you can from them. Then came anger, greed, resentment, and the bad relationships. All these things have led to this existence. You cry out "No!" It's too much for you to bear, so we run back to the machine. "That wasn't me," you try to convince yourself, but that's the thing: nobody ever thinks it will be them in prison or in addiction or in any horrible condition, but that's where bad choices lead.

Needing to get away from you, we press another button that leads to a different probability. The same things happen. The machine vibrates with a high pitch noise and shortly after stops. We open the door to another room. It's brighter, a light green color. We soon realize that we're in a hospital room. There's an old man on the bed hooked up to a breathing apparatus with tubes going into his arms. An overhead monitor measures his heart beat, oxygen level and blood pressure. Suddenly, the machine starts to beep loudly as his heart races. He just realized that it's you, and you realize that it's you. You stare at each other. Again, he explains that your choices have led to you spending the last ten years of your life suffering in poor health. You are in constant pain. There's no more joy in life. You're too weak to get out of bed and are dependent on others for your every need. You tell you that you should have taken care of yourself. You should have stopped smoking and drinking. You should have watched what you ate. You stare in disbelief at this poor soul. It's too much for you to take, so you run back to the machine.

Again the machine starts to vibrate and shake. The noise is deafening, but thankfully only lasts for about a minute before we stop again. This time we open the door cautiously. You're afraid of what you might see. This time we're standing behind a man in pajamas sitting in a lunch room. It looks like a retirement home. He's sitting all alone. We sit next to him and he looks at you. He knows who you are. You are him, but he doesn't want to talk. This time it's you who wants to do all the talking.

"Where's my family?" you ask. "Where is everyone? Why are we alone?" But he doesn't answer because he knows that you know. You've wasted your life. You've let the circumstances of your life stop you. With tears flowing down your face, you head back to the machine. "Let's go to the probabilities of the good choices," you say, and with that the machine starts again.

As it stops this time, you open the door slowly and peer around the corner. Instantly, you know you are in a good place. You are in a beautiful home. You see yourself sitting comfortably on your sofa, with your wife sitting next to you talking about the grandkids and their next visit. They suddenly look up and see you. With gratitude in their voices, they invite you to sit with them. They thank you for all the right choices you made and for all the sacrifices you made that led them to this place. They show you all the photos on the wall of your kids and grandkids. There are pictures of vacations and camping trips, Christmas family get-togethers, baseball games, and all sorts of outings. The other wall boasts achievement awards and appreciation certificates. Your future self has a loving spouse and family and has lived a full life and is still vibrant. There's a sparkle in his eye and a spring to his step, and he continues to live every day excited about what God is going to bring his way.

Sowing and reaping are all about making decisions and choices. Learn to sow seeds of good deeds, acts of kindness, righteousness, and healthy living. Treat people with honesty, integrity, and respect. Be kind and loving. Work hard and do more than is expected. Be honorable and of good character. Treat your body well. Eat good food and exercise. Never stop learning. After you have done all this, rest in God and see Him bring the harvest in due time. The beautiful thing about the harvest is that it's always far greater than what was sown. From one seed you will get multiplied fruit!

Here's to your amazing harvest!

Chapter 16
YOUR EULOGY

"Whoever pursues righteousness and love finds life, prosperity and honor"

(Proverbs 21:21)

A story is told of two wicked brothers. It seems they had swindled and taken advantage of everybody in their small town. They were known for their dishonesty and shrewd dealings. They caused tremendous hardships for everyone they met. One day the younger brother died suddenly, and the older brother went to see the pastor of the church where the funeral would be held. He promised the pastor a large sum of money if in the eulogy he would say that his brother was a "saint." The pastor had quite the dilemma, as the church really needed the money but to say this man was a saint would have been outrageous to say the least. In addition, the pastor would have lost tremendous respect from his congregation if he ever said such a thing. The day of the funeral came and the little church was packed, as the parishioners had heard of the pastor's dilemma and wanted to see how he would handle the situation. As the service began, the pastor stood up and said the usual prayers and required rites of the church and then started the eulogy.

He pointed to the man in the coffin and said, "He was a much-despised man because he robbed and cheated everyone he had ever met. There wasn't an ounce of kindness anywhere in his heart, but compared to his brother sitting there in the front row, the deceased was a saint!"

This pastor's predicament is a cute little anecdote, but the truth in it is that your life is your story. The great news is that you can write your own eulogy now. Don't leave it to others to try to find kind words to describe your accomplishments and the goodness of your life.

Don't wait until you're on your death bed and think back with regrets on what could have been. If only you had loved more, spent more time with your loved ones, been kinder to the people in your life, and pursued your dreams. Don't wait until it's too late. There's nothing sadder than a life looked back upon with regrets.

Don't let your circumstances dictate what kind of life you live. You can rise above any hardship, any challenge, and any handicap. Like I said earlier, it's those very challenges that will make your accomplishments great, which will make you great! This book has been written to encourage you, but you need to make the decision … and only you can make it for yourself.

How do you want to be remembered? How do you want to live your life? What difference is your life making? Who are you impacting? What changes do you need to make to live the life you want and the life you want to be remembered for? These are great questions. Write them down in your journal and honestly answer them. Make the changes necessary to achieve the life you dream of. Put the principles in this book to work for you. Live a life of faithfulness and forgiveness and do the small things with enthusiasm. Think critically and live courageously. Be grateful and generous and, above all, love deeply!

Write your own eulogy by living the life you dream of and be amazing!

Action plan

"Faith without works is dead"
(James 2:7, paraphrased)

You may believe that everything you've just read is good and true and that these principles work. However, without putting those principles into practice, this book is just a collection of words and stories and will be of no benefit to you.

They say that to make a habit, whether good or bad, takes about three weeks. It takes another three weeks to solidify the habit. During the next three weeks, start to make these principles a habit so that they become a way of life for you. Then do it again as you make more changes. Continue making good habits. Make it a habit to continue to learn. Make it a habit to continue to grow in all areas of your life. This book is purposely small and simple and easy to navigate. The only tool that I strongly suggest is a journal to help you put your thoughts on paper. A journal will also help you measure your successes! The exercise of writing your thoughts down is very powerful, as it makes a commitment in your brain.

Go through this book again and work through it using your journal. Pray and write down your ideas, thoughts, and goals. Then put these principles to work for you. Start again in Chapter One, "The Principle of Choice." This is exactly what is says: you get to choose your life. Then on to Chapter Two, "The Principle of Forgiveness." This too you must choose. You must choose to have faith, but not blind faith. There must be understanding and truth. You must choose to have faith in God and to accept His forgiveness. You must choose to repent and to leave your ways that are hindering your relationship with God. You must choose to forgive those who hurt you. Then choose to go the extra mile and so on through the principles. These principles are a step by step process. To do all this you must use your mind. This is the common denominator in all the principles. You must use your mind, think critically, and employ choice and decision. Decide today to have an amazing life.

Here's to your amazing life!

Printed in Canada